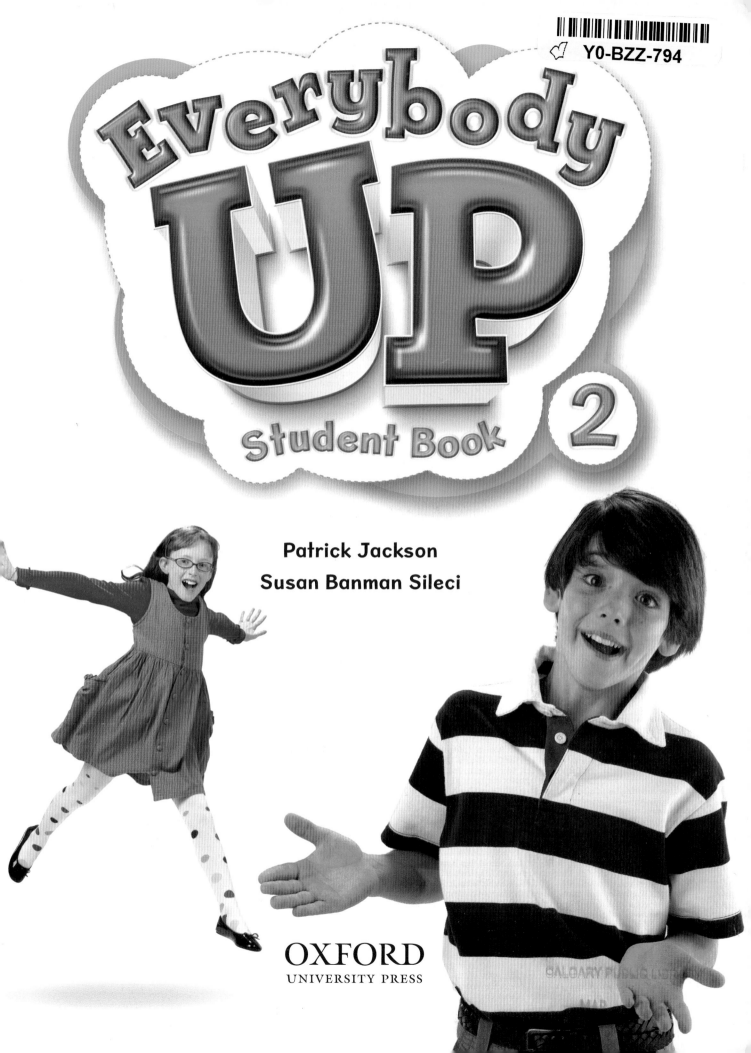

Everybody UP
Student Book 2

Patrick Jackson
Susan Banman Sileci

OXFORD
UNIVERSITY PRESS

Y0-BZZ-794

OXFORD
UNIVERSITY PRESS

198 Madison Avenue
New York, NY 10016 USA

Great Clarendon Street, Oxford OX2 6DP UK

Oxford University Press is a department of the University of Oxford.
It furthers the University's objective of excellence in research, scholarship,
and education by publishing worldwide in

Oxford   New York

Auckland   Cape Town   Dar es Salaam   Hong Kong   Karachi
Kuala Lumpur   Madrid   Melbourne   Mexico City   Nairobi
New Delhi   Shanghai   Taipei   Toronto

With offices in

Argentina   Austria   Brazil   Chile   Czech Republic   France   Greece
Guatemala   Hungary   Italy   Japan   Poland   Portugal   Singapore
South Korea   Switzerland   Thailand   Turkey   Ukraine   Vietnam

OXFORD and OXFORD ENGLISH are registered trademarks of
Oxford University Press in certain countries.

© Oxford University Press 2012

Database right Oxford University Press (maker)

No unauthorized photocopying

All rights reserved. No part of this publication may be reproduced,
stored in a retrieval system, or transmitted, in any form or by any means,
without the prior permission in writing of Oxford University Press, or as
expressly permitted by law, or under terms agreed with the appropriate
copyright clearance organization. Enquiries concerning reproduction
outside the scope of the above should be sent to the ELT Rights Department,
Oxford University Press, at the address above.

You must not circulate this book in any other binding or cover
and you must impose this same condition on any acquirer.

Any websites referred to in this publication are in the public domain and
their addresses are provided by Oxford University Press for information only.
Oxford University Press disclaims any responsibility for the content.

General Manager, American ELT: Laura Pearson
Executive Publishing Manager: Shelagh Speers
Managing Editor: Clare Hambly
Art, Design, and Production Director: Susan Sanguily
Design Manager: Lisa Donovan
Senior Designer: Molly K. Scanlon
Image Manager: Trisha Masterson
Image Editor: Fran Newman
Production Coordinator: Hila Ratzabi
Senior Manufacturing Controller: Eve Wong

ISBN: 978-0-19-410337-4 Student Book with Audio CD
ISBN: 978-0-19-410338-1 Student Book as pack component
ISBN: 978-0-19-410339-8 Audio CD as pack component

Printed in China

This book is printed on paper from certified and well-managed sources.

10 9 8 7 6 5 4

ACKNOWLEDGMENTS

Oxford University Press would like to thank the thousands of teachers whose
opinions helped to inform this series, and in particular, the following reviewers:

Ayoub Ait Ali, Ministry of Education, Casablanca, Morocco; **Michael P. Bassett**,
Osaka International School, Osaka, Japan; **Paul Richard Batt**, Elephant's Memory
Learning Institute, Taichung; **Jawida Ben Afia**, Inspector General for Education, Tunis,
Tunisia; **Clara Lee Brown**, University of Tennessee, Knoxville, USA; **Dana Buck**,
Margaret Institute of Language (MIL), Chiba, Japan; **Roberta Calderbank**, Educational
Consultant, Riyadh, Saudi Arabia; **Whoisuk Jackie Che**, Hankuk University of Foreign
Studies, Seoul, Korea; **Yuwen Catherine Chen**, Eden Language Institute, Taichung;
Young-ae Chung, International Graduate School of English, Seoul, Korea; **Cláudia
Colla de Amorim**, Escola Móbile, São Paulo, Brazil; **Grace Costa de Oliveira**, Colégio
Franciscano Nossa Senhora Aparecida, São Paulo, Brazil; **Simon R. Downes**, Simon
BEAR School (Bilingual Education and Reasearch), Tokyo, Japan; **Elaine Elia**, Escola
Caminho Aberto, São Paulo, Brazil; **Mark Evans**, Wisdom Bank Language School,
Kaohsiung; **Sean Gallagher**, Happy English Club, Inc., Nagoya, Japan; **Tania Garcia**,
Montessori Santa Terezinha, São Paulo, Brazil; **Patricia Gazzi**, Cristo Rei School, São
Paulo, Brazil; **Keith Grehan**, Mosaica Education, Abu Dhabi, United Arab Emirates;
Anna Kyungmi Han, EB (English Break) Language School, Paju, Korea; **Briony Hewitt**,
ILA Vietnam, Ho Chi Minh City, Vietnam; **Kelly Hsu**, Kelly English School, Taichung;
Kyla KCW Huang, Kang Ning English School, Hsinchu; **Lilian Itzicovitch Leventhal**,
Colegio I.L. Peretz, São Paulo, Brazil; **Aaron Jolly**, Hanseo University, Seosan, Korea;
Sean Pan-Seob Kim, Kangseo Wonderland, Seoul, Korea; **Charlotte Lee**, Jordan's
Language School Headquarters, Taipei; **Hsiang-pao Sarah Lin**, Lincoln International
Language School, Tainan; **David Martin**, Busy Beavers English Resources, Vancouver,
Canada; **Conrad Matsumoto**, Conrad's English House, Odawara, Japan; **Daniel McNeill**,
Yokohama YMCA, Yokohama, Japan; **Sung Hee Park**, Yonsei University Graduate
School of Education, Anyang, Korea; **Sandra Puccioni Katsuda**, Colégio Montessori
Santa Terezinha, São Paulo, Brazil; **Saba'a Qhadi**, University of Qatar, Doha, Qatar;
Juliana Queiroz Pereira, Colégio Marista Arquidiocesano and Colégio I. L. Peretz,
São Paulo, Brazil; **Karyna Ribeiro**, Colégio Miguel de Cervantes, São Paulo, Brazil;
Charlie Richards, The Learning Tree English School, Osaka, Japan; **Mark Riley**,
Shane English School, Taipei; **John Sanders**, Camelot English Study Centre, Tokyo,
Japan; **Kaj Schwermer**, Eureka Learning Institute, Osaka, Japan; **Monika Soens Yang**,
Taipei European School, Taipei; **Jiyeon Song**, Seoul, Korea; **Jason Stewart**, Taejeon
International Language School, Daejeon, Korea; **David Stucker**, Myojo Elementary
School, Beppu, Japan; **Andrew Townshend**, Natural English School, Tokyo, Japan;
Thanaphong Udomsab, Petchaburi Rajabhat University, Petchaburi, Thailand; **Aliéte
Mara Ventura**, Escola Carandá, São Paulo, Brazil; **Ariel Yao**, Ren Da English School,
Taipei.

Cover Design: Molly K. Scanlon

Illustrations by: Ken Batelman: 18-19 (top 4 buildings, town); Charlene Chua: 2, 4 (bot.), 6
(bot.), 8, 9 (top), 12, 14, 16, 17 (top), 22, 24, 26, 27 (top), 30, 32, 34, 35 (top), 40, 42, 44, 45
(top), 48, 50 (bot.), 52, 53 (top), 58 (bot.), 60 (bot.), 62, 63 (top), 66 (bot.), 68 (bot.), 70, 71
(top); Andy Elkerton: 5, 10, 11, 17 (border, bot.), 25, 31, 38 (mid.), 39, 45 (border, bot.),
64 (top, bot. scenes), 71 (bot.), 74; Ken Gamage: 36 (top ice), 49 (mid., bot.), 50 (top), 51,
58 (top), 59, 60 (top), 61, 72 (top); Nathan Hale: 18 (4 people spots), 19, 36-37, 72 (bot.);
Jannie Ho: 6 (top), 7, 13, 20 (mid.), 21, 27 (border, bot.), 33 (top, border), 41, 49 (top), 63
(border, bot.), 68 (top), 69, 74 (mid.), 75; Nathan Jarvis: 3, 4 (top), 9 (border, bot.), 15,
23, 28 (bot.), 29 (top), 35 (border, bot.), 43, 53 (border, bot.), 56 (mid.), 57, 66 (top), 67, 71
(border), 74; John Kurtz: (kid drawn art) 37, 51; Rob Schuster: 28-29 (barn, background,
milk box), 46 (cameras), 54, 55, 64 (houses), 65 (chart).

Commissioned photography by: Richard Hutchings/Digital Light Source, Cover photos
and all photos of kids in lower right-hand corner of pages: 2, 5, 7, 9, 11, 13, 15, 17,
19, 23, 25, 27, 29, 31, 33, 35, 37, 41, 43, 45, 47, 49, 51, 53, 55, 59, 61, 63, 65, 67, 69,
71, 73 and the following articles of clothing: 30 (shirt, dress and pants), 32 (shorts);
Gareth Boden, pg. 30 (socks), pg. 61 (boy); Paul Bricknell, pg. 32 (sneakers); Dennis
Kitchen Studio, Inc., pg 32 (T-shirt); David Jordan, pg. 48 (clock); Mark Mason: pg. 24
(banana), pg. 28 (milk), pg. 28 (yogurt), pg. 29 (boy), pg. 31 (boy). Pg. 31 (girl).

*The publishers would like to thank the following for their kind permission to reproduce
photographs:* Franz Marc Frei/LOOK/Getty Images, pg. 10 (Oktoberfest); UpperCut, pg.
12 (female doctor); Digital Vision, pg. 12 (hospital bkgd); ©Yuri Arcurs/Shutterstock.
com, pg. 12 (nurse); WR Publishing, pg. 12 (hospital bkgd); Tetra Images/Jupiter
Images, pg. 12 (teacher); Photodisc, pg. 12 (student): ©Redchopsticks.com/Alamy, pg.
12 (pilot); Somos, pg. 12 (cook); Corbis/Digital Stock, pg. 13 (doctor); Digital Vision, pg.
13 (nurse); Blend Images, pg. 13 (teacher); Digital Vision, pg. 13 (student); Fuse/Getty
Images, pg. 13 (pilot); Photodisc, pg. 13 (female cook); UpperCut Images/Getty Images,
pg. 14 (police officer); Getty Images/Jupiterimages, pg. 14 (female firefighter); Brand
X Pictures/Jupiter Images, pg. 14 (bus driver); Corbis/Jupiter Images, pg. 14 (soccer
player); ©gualtiero boffi/Shutterstock.com, pg. 18 (blueprint pattern); bphillips/
iStockphoto, pg. 22 (soup); ©Dino O./Shutterstock.com, pg. 22 (salad); ©Michele
Cozzolino/Shutterstock.com, pg. 22 (spaghetti); Creatas / Comstock, pg. 22 (fries);
Photodisc, pg. 22 (steak); ©Analia Valeria Urani/Shutterstock.com, pg. 22 (eggs); ©Alex
Staroseltsev/Shutterstock.com, pg. 24 (apple); ©Max Krasnov/Shutterstock.com, pg.
24 (orange); © Sebastian Kaulitzki/Shutterstock.com, pg. 24 (peach); ©igor kisselev/
Shutterstock.com, pg. 28 (cheese behind a,b,c,d); ©Gregory Gerber/Shutterstock.
com, pg. 28 (cheese); Tetra Images/Jupiter Images, pg. 28 (butter); Geoff du Feu, pg.
29 (girl 1); Claudia Rehm/Jupiter Images, pg. 29 (girl 2); Imageshop, pg. 29 (boy 2); ©
maxstockphoto/Shutterstock.com, pg. 30 (skirt); ©Rick's Photography/Shutterstock.
com, pg. 30 (shoes); Digital Vision/Getty Images, pg. 31 (boy 2); JGI/Jamie Grill/
Jupiter Images, pg. 31 (girl 2); Photodisc, pg. 32 (cap); ©Getty Images/liquidlibrary/
Jupiterimages, pg. 36 (hat): lepas2004/iStockphoto, pg. 36 (coat); ©Brian Chase/
Shutterstock.com, pg. 36 (sweater); ©Ingvald Kaldhussater/Shutterstock.com, pg. 36
(boots); Masterfile (Royalty-Free Div.), pg. 37 (boy 1); Pauline St. Denis/AgeFotostock,
pg. 37 (girl 1); MIXA/AgeFotostock, pg. 37 (girl 2); Picture Contact / Alamy, pg. 37
(eskimo boy); Mark Edward Atkinson/Blend Images/Jupiter Images, pg. 40 (boy 1);
JGI/Blend Images/Jupiter Images, pg. 40 (girl 1); Masterfile (Royalty-Free Div.), pg. 40
(boy 2); Deborah Jaffe/Jupiter Images, pg. 40 (girl 2); Oppenheim Bernhard/Jupiter
Images, pg. 40 (boy 3); BOLD STOCK/AgeFotostock, pg. 40 (girl 3); Masterfile (Royalty-
Free Div.), pg. 42 (girl 1); Pixland/Jupiterimages, pg. 42 (boy 1); Photodisc, pg. 42 (boy
2); Celia Peterson/Getty Images, pg. 42 (boy 3); Masterfile (Royalty-Free Div.), pg. 46
(play the guitar); ©Corbis Super RF / Alamy, pg. 46 (listen to music); © OJO Images
Ltd / Alamy, pg. 46 (watch tv); Jamie Grill/Jupiter Images, pg. 46 (do homework);
George Doyle/Jupiter Images, pg. 46 (boy playing guitar); Ariel Skelley/AgeFotostock,
pg. 46 (girls listening to mp3 player); Jose Luis Pelaez, Inc/AgeFotostock, pg. 46 (girls
watching television); Jose Luis Pelaez, Inc/AgeFotostock, pg. 46 (girl doing homework);
Image Source/Jupiter Images, pg. 47 (boy writing in a notebook); Brand X Pictures/
Jupiterimages, pg. 47 (girl holding microphone); ©MBI / Alamy, pg. 47 (brother/
sister eating lunch); TOPIC PHOTO AGENCY IN/AgeFotostock, pg. 47 (girls reading);
© Mouse in the House / Alamy, pg. 48 (bed); © BUILT Images / Alamy, pg. 48 (book
shelf); ©Simon Krzic/iStockphoto, pg. 48 (table); ©fckncg/Shutterstock.com, pg. 48
(sofa); Tetra Images, pg. 48 (computer); Photodisc, pg. 61 (girl); Alan Bailey/Rubberball/
Jupiter Images, pg. 65 (boy); Photodisc, pg. 69 (girl); Photodisc, pg. 69 (boy); ©kak2s/
Shutterstock.com, pg. 72-73 (globe background); ©dbimages / Alamy, pg. 73 (boy);
Banana Stock/AgeFotostock, pg. 73 (girl 1); ©TongRo Image Stock / Alamy, pg. 73 (girl
2); Caterina Bernardi/Jupiter Images, pg. 73 (boy 2).

Music by:
Julie Gold: 3, 43, 45, 61, 63
Red Grammer: 15, 17, 51, 53
Troy McDonald and Devon Thagard: 33,35, 69, 71
Ilene Weiss: 7, 9, 25, 27

For darling Kai. My main guy. Now let's make up for all those times when
I told you to leave me alone because I was too busy.

—P.J.

For my wonderful family—Riccardo, Audrey, and Natalie.

—S.B.S.

Table of Contents

Welcome 2

Unit 1 **How We Feel** 4
Unit 2 **In Town** 12
    Review 1 20
    Phonics 1 21

Unit 3 **Things to Eat** 22
Unit 4 **Things to Wear** 30
    Review 2 38
    Phonics 2 39

Unit 5 **Things to Do** 40
Unit 6 **Home** 48
    Review 3 56
    Phonics 3 57

Unit 7 **My Day** 58
Unit 8 **My Week** 66
    Review 4 74
    Phonics 4 75

Syllabus 76

Word List 78

Welcome

A **Listen, read, and say.** CD1 03

1. My name is Danny. I'm eight. I have a sister. I like green. I like pizza. I don't like green pizza!

Danny

2. 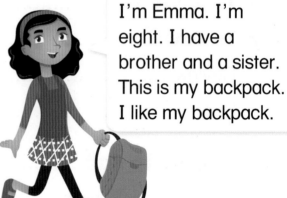 I'm Emma. I'm eight. I have a brother and a sister. This is my backpack. I like my backpack.

Emma

3.  My name is Julie. I'm nine. I have two brothers. I can play soccer. I like soccer.

Julie

4.  I'm Mike. I'm nine. I have a brother. I have a bike. I like my bike. It's fast!

Mike

B **What about you? Talk with your classmates.**

C Sing. CD1 04

The Days of the Week						
Sunday	Monday	Tuesday	Wednesday	Thursday	Friday	Saturday

What day is it today?
It's Sunday. It's Sunday.
Today is Sunday.
There are seven days
in the week.

What day is it today?
It's Monday. It's Monday.
Today is Monday.
There are seven days
in the week.

03

D Listen, point, and say. CD1 05

1.
Read.

2.
Write.

3.
T-R-E-E
Spell.

4.
Come to the board.

5.
Open your book.

6.
Close your book.

04

3

1 How We Feel

A Listen, point, and say. CD1 06

1	2	3	4	5	6

happy	sad	hot	cold	hungry	thirsty

05

B Listen and find. CD1 07

C Listen and say. Then practice.

I'm happy. I'm not sad. | I'm = I am

1.  2.  3.  4.  5.  6.

D Listen, ask, and answer. Then practice.

Are you happy?   Yes, I am.
                  No, I'm not.

I'm happy!

E Look at B. Point, ask, and answer.

Are you thirsty?

Yes, I am.

A Listen, point, and say. CD1 10

| sick | tired | bored | excited |

06

B Listen and say. Then practice. CD1 11

He's
She's | sick.

He's = He is
She's = She is

C Listen, ask, and answer. Then practice.

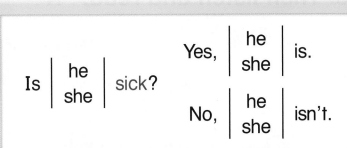

| Is | he / she | sick? | Yes, | he / she | is. |
| | | | No, | he / she | isn't. |

isn't = is not

1.
2.
3.
4.

D Chant.

Sick, Tired, Bored, Excited

She isn't sick.   She isn't sick.

He's sick.   He's sick.

She isn't sick.   She is tired. She isn't sick.

He's sick.   He's sick.

07

E Act. Ask and answer.

Is she tired?

Yes, she is.

I'm excited!
What about you?

A Talk about the pictures. Then listen and read.

Are You OK?

B Listen and number. CD1 15

C Sing. CD1 16

Are You OK?

Oops. Ouch!

What's wrong? Are you OK? Are you OK?

What's wrong? Are you OK? Are you OK?

Ouch! My leg hurts. Ouch! My leg hurts.

Are you OK? Are you OK?

Ouch! I think so. Oh! I think so. Yes! I think so. Thanks!

  08

D Listen and say. Then act. CD1 17

Ouch!

What's wrong?

My leg hurts.

leg

2

hand

3

finger

Are you OK?

A Listen, point, and say. CD1 18

see

hear

smell

taste

touch

09

B Listen, ask, and answer. Then practice. CD1 19

| What can | he
she | see? | He
She | can see a bird. |

a ball   a bird
a car   a dog
a doll   a flower
a kite   ice cream
juice   pizza

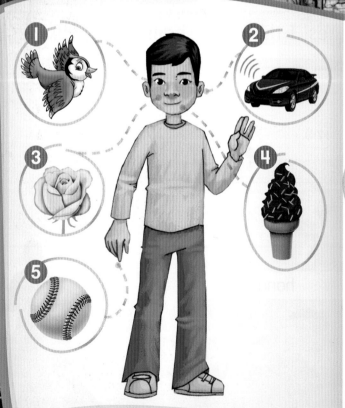

C Listen. Fill in the charts. (CD1 20)

a bus	a dog
a flower	a pen
bread	pizza

	👁	👂	👃	👅	✋
(pen)	✓				
(bread)					
(dog)					

	👁	👂	👃	👅	✋
(pizza)					
(bus)					
(flower)					

What can you see?

D Look at C.
Point, ask, and answer.

What can she see?

She can see a pen.

Lesson 1 | Jobs

A Listen, point, and say. CD1 21

1	2	3	4	5	6
doctor	nurse	teacher	student	pilot	cook

10

B Listen and find. CD1 22

Welcome

C Listen and say. Then practice. 🔊 CD1 23

| He's She's | a doctor. | He She | isn't a nurse. |

He's = He is
She's = She is
isn't = is not

1.  2.  3.  4.  5.  6.

D Listen, ask, and answer. Then practice. 🔊 CD1 24

| Is | he she | a doctor? | Yes, | he she | is. | | |
| | | | No, | he she | isn't. | He's She's | a nurse. |

E Look at B. Point, ask, and answer. 🔊

Is she a pilot?

Yes, she is.

My father is a teacher.

A Listen, point, and say. CD1 25

1	2	3	4
police officer	firefighter	bus driver	soccer player

B Listen and say. Then practice. CD1 26

They're police officers. They aren't firefighters.

They're = They are
aren't = are not

police officers   firefighters   bus drivers   soccer players

STOP

C Listen, ask, and answer. Then practice.

| Are they police officers? | Yes, they are.
No, they aren't. They're firefighters. |

1.  2.  3.  4.

D Chant.

Yes, They Are

Are they police officers?

Yes, they are.

Are they firefighters?

No, they aren't.

They're police officers.

Are they soccer players?

Yes, they are.

Are they bus drivers?

No, they aren't.

They're soccer players.

12

E Draw and write. Show and tell.

They're firefighters.

My brothers
are soccer
players.

They're firefighters.

A Talk about the pictures. Then listen and read.

Oh, Danny

B Listen and number. CD1 30

C Sing. CD1 31

May I Borrow Your Phone?

Excuse me. May I borrow your phone?

Sure. Here you are.

Thanks!

You're welcome!

Please may I borrow your phone?

Sure! Here you are.

13

D Listen and say. Then act. CD1 32

Excuse me. May I borrow your phone?

Sure. Here you are.

Thanks.

1

phone

2

pen

3

marker

Look at me!

Lesson 4 **Places**

Social Studies

A Listen, point, and say. CD1 33

1. hospital
2. school
3. home
4. restaurant 14

B Listen, ask, and answer. Then practice. CD1 34

Where's the doctor? He's / She's at the hospital.

Where's = Where is
He's = He is
She's = She is

at home   at the hospital
at school   at the restaurant

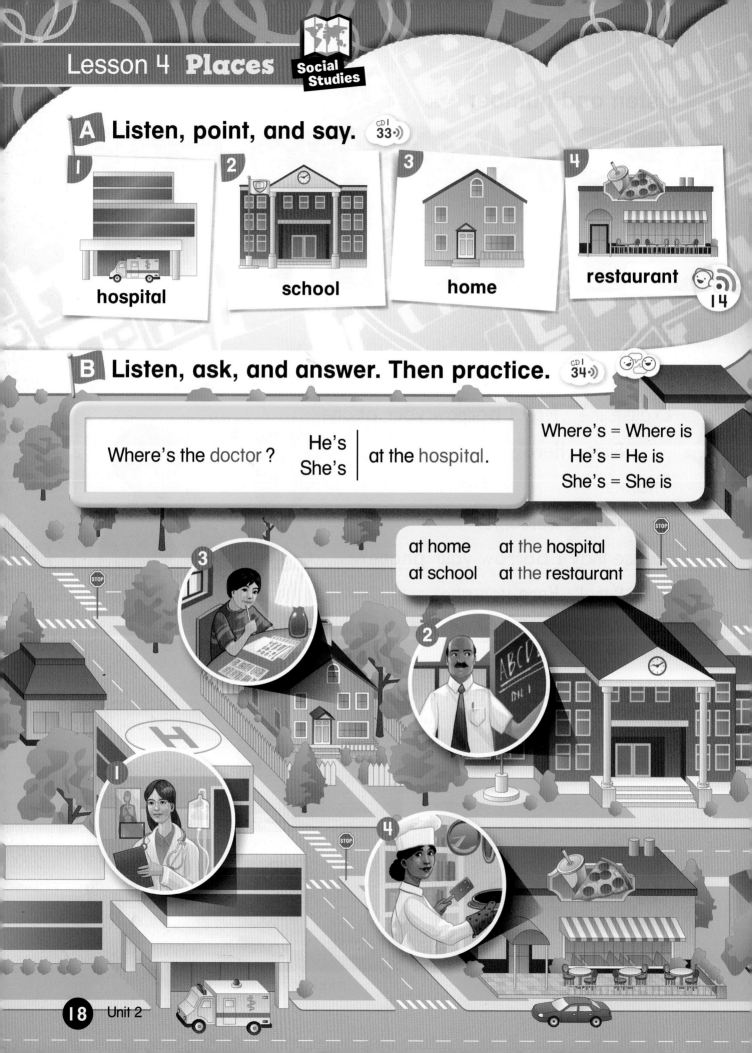

18 Unit 2

C Listen and number. CD1 35·))

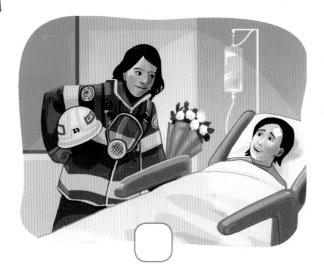

D Look at **C**.
Ask and answer.

Where's the firefighter?

She's at the hospital.

I'm at school.
Where are you?

Review 1

A I can say these words.

1.
2.
3.
4.
5.
6.
7.
8.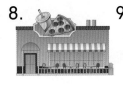
9.
10.
11.
12.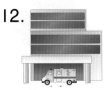

B I can talk about these topics.

1.
feelings

2.
the senses

3.
jobs

4.
places

C I can talk with you.

1.

Ouch!

My hand hurts.

2.
Sure. Here you are.

Phonics

A Listen, point, and say. CD1 36

cave

c cub

girl g game

jam j jug

hippo h hose

king k kitten

6 six x box

15

B Look at A. Point and read with your partner.

C Listen and read. CD1 37

1.

The girl is in the cave.

2.

The hippo is on the jug.

3.

I can see six kittens.

3 Things to Eat

A **Listen, point, and say.** CD1 38

1	2	3	4	5	6
soup	salad	spaghetti	french fries	steak	eggs

16

B **Listen and find.** CD1 39

Menu

C Listen and say. Then practice. CD1 40))

| I | want / don't want | soup. | He / She | wants / doesn't want | soup. |

don't = do not
doesn't = does not

1. 2. 3.

D Listen, ask, and answer. Then practice. CD1 41))

| What do you want? | I want soup. |

| What does | he / she | want? | He / She | wants soup. |

1 2 3 4 5 6

E Look at B. Point, ask, and answer.

What does he want?

He wants steak.

I want spaghetti.
What do you want?

Lesson 2 Fruit

A Listen, point, and say. CD1 42

1	2	3	4
apple	banana	orange	peach

17

B Listen and say. Then practice. CD1 43

I	have don't have	apples.

He She	has doesn't have	apples.

don't = do not
doesn't = does not

apples   bananas
oranges   peaches

1   2   3   4

C Listen, ask, and answer. Then practice.

| | Do you have apples? | Yes, I do.
No, I don't. | | | |

| Does | he
she | have apples? | Yes, | he
she | does. |
| | | | No, | he
she | doesn't. |

1.
2.
3.
4.

D Sing.

Does She Have Apples?

Does she have apples?   Yes, she does.

Does she have peaches?   Yes, she does.

Does she have oranges?   Yes, she does.

Does she have bananas?   No, she doesn't.

18

E Draw pictures. Ask and answer.

Does she have oranges?

No, she doesn't.

My teacher has an apple.

A **Talk about the pictures. Then listen and read.**

Yes, Please

B Listen and number.

C Sing. 🔊

Do You Want an Apple?

Do you want an apple?

Yes!   No!

Excuse me? Excuse me?

Do you want an apple?

Yes, please!   No. No, thank you!

19

D Listen and say. Then act. 🔊

Do you want an apple?

Yes, please.

No, thank you.

Do you want an orange?

apple

banana

peach

Lesson 4 Dairy Products

Science

A Listen, point, and say. CD1 50

1 milk
2 yogurt
3 cheese
4 butter

20

B Listen, ask, and answer. Then practice. CD1 51

Do you like milk?   Yes, I do.
                     No, I don't.

don't = do not

C Listen and match. CD1 52 🔊

1. Matt •

2. Kathy •

3. Jenny •

4. Sam •

D What about you and your partner?
Ask and answer. 😊

Do you like yogurt? I do!

	Me	My Partner
milk		
cheese		
yogurt		
butter		

Do you like cheese?

Yes, I do.

4 Things to Wear

A Listen, point, and say. CD1 53

1	2	3	4	5	6

shirt	dress	skirt	pants	socks	shoes

21

B Listen and find. CD1 54

C Listen and say. Then practice.  CD1 55·))

| He's / She's | wearing a shirt. |

He's = He is
She's = She is

a shirt   a dress
a skirt   pants
socks   shoes

1.  2.  3.  4.  5.  6.

D Listen, ask, and answer. Then practice. CD1 56·))

| What's | he / she | wearing? |

He's / She's | wearing a white shirt and gray pants.

What's = What is

1.  2.  3.  4.

What's your
friend
wearing?

E Look at B. Point, ask, and answer.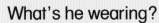

What's he wearing?

He's wearing a yellow
shirt and green pants.

Lesson 1 **31**

A Listen, point, and say. CD1 57

1	2	3	4
cap	T-shirt	shorts	sneakers

22

B Listen and say. Then practice. CD1 58

I'm We're	wearing	a cap. caps.

I'm = I am
We're = We are

a cap   caps
a T-shirt   T-shirts
shorts   sneakers

C Listen, ask, and answer. Then practice.

What are you wearing?			
I'm We're	wearing	a red cap red caps	and green shorts.

1.

2.

3.

4.

D Sing. CD1 60

My Clothes

I'm wearing a blue T-shirt.
I'm wearing orange shorts.
I'm wearing green sneakers
and a red cap on my head.

23

E Talk with your classmates. Ask and answer.

What are you wearing?

What are you wearing?

I'm wearing a black T-shirt and white shorts.

A Talk about the pictures. Then listen and read.

Where's Mom?

B Listen and number. CD1 62

C Sing. CD1 63

What's Your Phone Number?

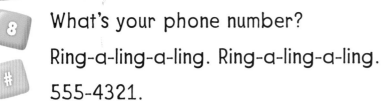
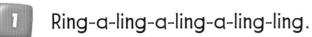

What's your phone number?

Ring-a-ling-a-ling. Ring-a-ling-a-ling.

555-4321.

Ring-a-ling-a-ling-a-ling-ling.

24

D Listen and say. Then act. CD1 64

What's your
phone number?

It's 829-3071.

1

829-3071

2

462-8153

3

697-3945

What's your
phone number?

A **Listen, point, and say.** CD1 65

1	2	3	4
hat	coat	sweater	boots

25

B **Listen, ask, and answer. Then practice.** CD1 66

| Is | he / she | wearing a hat? | Yes, | he / she | is. |
| | | | No, | he / she | isn't. |

isn't = is not

a hat
a coat
a sweater
boots

C Look at the pictures. Circle.

1	2	3	4
(T-shirt)	cap	dress	sneakers
hat	skirt	sweater	coat
boots	shorts	shoes	boots
shorts	sweater	socks	skirt
skirt	boots	skirt	pants

D Look at C.
Ask and answer.

She's wearing a coat and a hat.

Is he wearing a sweater?

No, he isn't.
He's wearing a T-shirt.

Review 2

Award

A I can say these words.

1.
2.
3.
4.
5.
6.

7.
8.
9.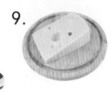
10.
11.
12.

B I can talk about these topics.

1.
food

2.
fruit

3.
dairy products

4.
clothes

C I can talk with you.

1.

Do you want a peach?

No, thank you.

2.

What's your phone number?

A Listen, point, and say. CD 67

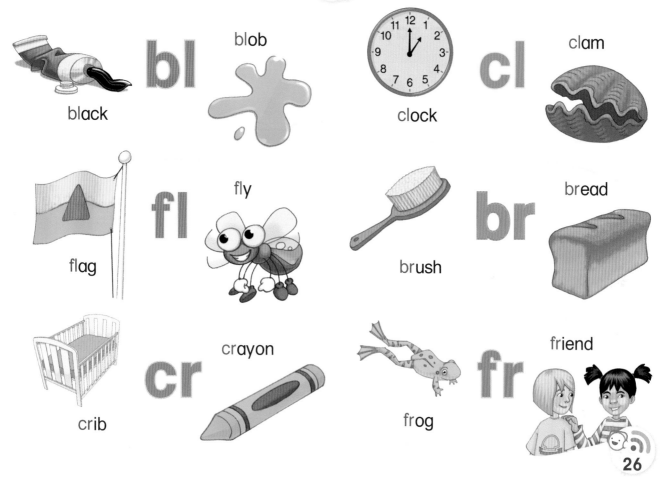

bl — black — blob

cl — clock — clam

fl — flag — fly

br — brush — bread

cr — crib — crayon

fr — frog — friend

26

B Look at A. Point and read with your partner.

C Listen and read. CDI 68

1.
This clam is black.

2.
My friend likes bread.

3.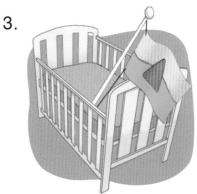
The flag is in the crib.

5 Things to Do

A Listen, point, and say. CD2 02

1	2	3	4	5	6

read	write	draw	talk	sing	dance

27

B Listen and find. CD2 03

C Listen and say. Then practice. CD2 04))

I'm		I'm not	
He's	reading.	He isn't	writing.
She's		She isn't	

I'm = I am
He's = He is
She's = She is
isn't = is not

reading
writing
drawing
talking
singing
dancing

1.  2.  3.  4.  5. 6.

D Listen, ask, and answer. Then practice. CD2 05))

What are you doing?	I'm reading.

What's	he / she	doing?	He's / She's	reading.

What's = What is

1.  2.  3.  4.  5.  6.

E Look at B. Point, ask, and answer.

I'm dancing!

What's he doing?

He's writing.

Lesson 2 Actions

A Listen, point, and say. CD2 06

1	2	3	4
eat	drink	sleep	play

28

B Listen and say. Then practice. CD2 07

| We're They're | eating. | We They | aren't drinking. |

We're = We are
They're = They are
aren't = are not

eating   drinking
sleeping playing

C Listen, ask, and answer. Then practice.

| What are | you they | doing? | We're They're | eating. |

1.  2.  3.  4.

D Sing. CD2 09

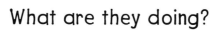
What Are You Doing?

What are you doing?

I am playing. I'm not sleeping.

I'm playing now.

What are they doing?

They are eating. They aren't drinking.

They're eating now.

29

E Draw pictures. Ask and answer.

I'm not sleeping!

What are they doing?

They're eating.

He | She | They

A Talk about the pictures. Then listen and read.

Let's Play!

Hi! I have a new game.

Mike, Danny's here.

Hi, Danny!

Good idea!

Let's play!

I'm bored. Can I play, too?

Oh, sure. I'm sorry.

What are you doing?

We're playing.

I'm winning!

Be nice.

B Listen and number. 🔊 CD2 11

C Sing. 🔊 CD2 12

Let's Play!

I'm bored. What are you doing?

We're playing.

Can I play, too?

Oh, sure. Good idea.

Let's play. Let's play.

30

D Listen and say. Then act. 🔊 CD2 13

Let's play!

Good idea!

1

play

2

eat

3

dance

Let's play!

Lesson 4 Activities

Art

A Listen, point, and say. CD2 14

play the guitar

listen to music

watch TV

do homework

31

B Listen, ask, and answer. Then practice. CD2 15

| Is | he she | playing the guitar? | Yes, | he she | is. |
| | | | No, | he she | isn't. |

| | Are they playing the guitar? | Yes, they are. |
| | | No, they aren't. |

isn't = is not
aren't = are not

playing the guitar
listening to music
watching TV
doing homework

My Photos

File   Edit   Print   Help

1.

2.

3.

4.

D Look at C. Point, ask, and answer.

Are they reading?

No, they aren't.
They're watching TV.

I'm listening to music!

E Make a poster.
Show and tell.

He's eating.

6 Home

A Listen, point, and say. CD2 17

1	2	3	4	5	6
bed	bookshelf	table	sofa	clock	computer

32

B Listen and find. CD2 18

C Listen and say. Then practice. CD2 19•))

There's a bed next to the bookshelf.

next to   in front of   behind

There's = There is

1.    2.   3.    4.   5.    6.

D Listen, ask, and answer. Then practice. CD2 20•))

Is there a bed next to the bookshelf?   Yes, there is.
No, there isn't.

isn't = is not

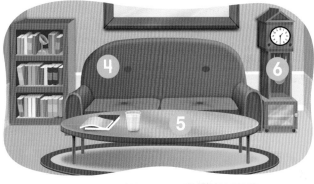

E Look at B.
Point, ask, and answer.

Is there a table in front of the bookshelf?

Yes, there is.

There's a computer next to my bed.

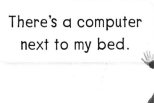

Lesson 2 Rooms

A Listen, point, and say. CD2 21

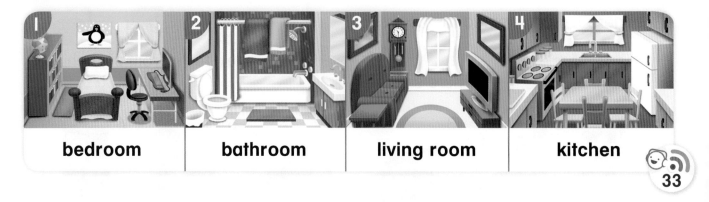

1	2	3	4
bedroom	bathroom	living room	kitchen

33

B Listen and say. Then practice. CD2 22

There's one bed
There are two beds | in the bedroom.

There's = There is

beds   clocks   chairs   sofas   bookshelves   tables

C Listen, ask, and answer. Then practice.

Are there two beds in the bedroom?

Yes, there are.
No, there aren't.

aren't = are not

1.

2.

3.

4.

D Sing.

  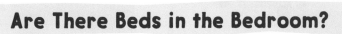

Are There Beds in the Bedroom?

Are there beds in the bedroom?	Yes, there are.
Are there chairs in the kitchen?	Yes, there are.
Are there bookshelves in the living room?	Yes, there are.
Are there bikes in the bedroom?	No, there aren't.
Are there sofas in the kitchen?	No, there aren't.
Are there beds in the bathroom?	No, there aren't.

34

E What about your home? Ask and answer.

Are there two beds in your bedroom?

Yes, there are.

This is my room.

A Talk about the pictures. Then listen and read.

Surprise!

The living room's messy!

Let's clean up.

OK.

There's a sock on the sofa!

There are books under the table!

What are they doing?

I don't know.

Wow!

Thank you!

Surprise!

Be helpful.

B Listen and number. CD2 26·))

C Sing. CD2 27·))

Let's Clean Up

The living room's messy!

    Let's clean up.   OK!

We have fingers. We have hands.

We can clean up. Yes, we can.

The living room's messy!

    Let's clean up.   OK!

 35

D Listen and say. Then act. CD2 28·))

The living room's messy!

Let's clean up.

OK.

living room

bathroom

classroom

Let's clean up!

Lesson 4 Numbers

 Math

A Listen, point, and say. CD2 29))

0 zero	1 one	2 two	3 three	4 four
5 five	6 six	7 seven	8 eight	9 nine
10 ten	11 eleven	12 twelve	13 thirteen	14 fourteen
15 fifteen	16 sixteen	17 seventeen	18 eighteen	19 nineteen
20 twenty	25 twenty-five	30 thirty	40 forty	50 fifty
60 sixty	70 seventy	80 eighty	90 ninety	100 one hundred

36

B Listen, ask, and answer. Then practice. CD2 30))

How many pencils are there?   There are 24 pencils.

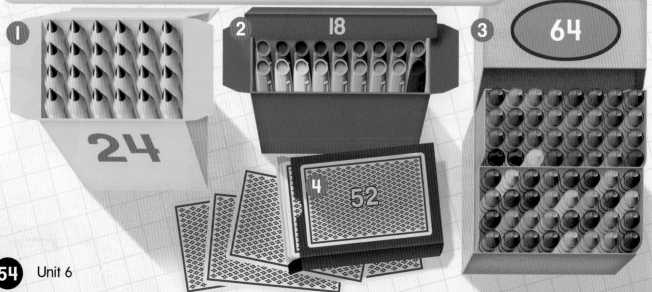

1 24

2 18

3 64

4 52

C **Count and write. Then listen and check.** CD2 31))

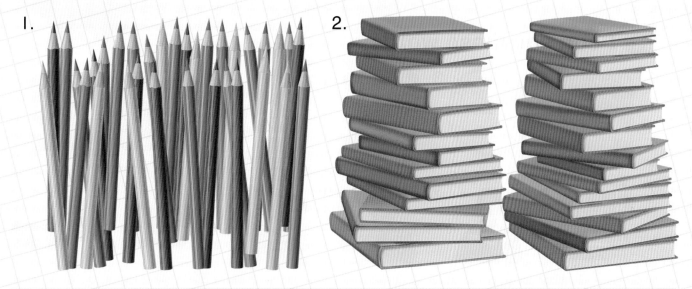

1.
2.

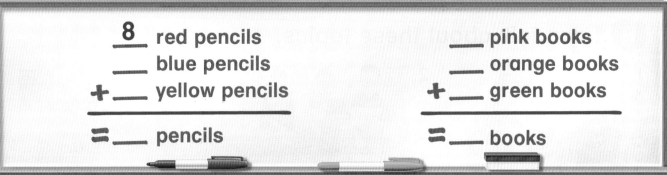

__8__ red pencils
___ blue pencils
+___ yellow pencils
_____
=___ pencils

___ pink books
___ orange books
+___ green books
_____
=___ books

D **Look at C. Ask and answer.**

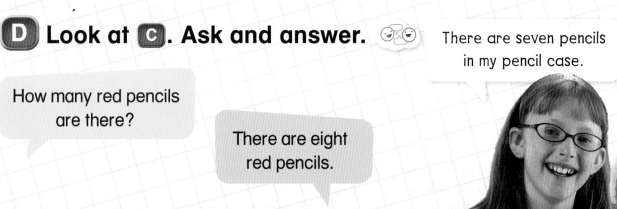

There are seven pencils in my pencil case.

How many red pencils are there?

There are eight red pencils.

E **What about your classroom?**
Ask and answer.

Review 3

A   I can say these words.

1.
2.
3.
4. **25**
5.
6.

7.
8.
9.
10.
11. **50**
12.

B   I can talk about these topics.

1.

actions

2.

activities

3.

things at home

4.

rooms

5.

numbers

C   I can talk with you.

1.

Let's eat!

2.

Let's clean up.

Phonics Bonus

A Listen, point, and say. CD2 32·))

 shell

sheep **sh**

 **ch**

chair

chin

 **th** think

three

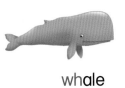 **wh**

whale

wheel

 ph

phone photo

37

B Look at A. Point and read with your partner.

C Listen and read. CD2 33·))

1.

2.

3.

The sheep is on the chair. The whale has a wheel. There are three phones.

Phonics 3 **57**

7 My Day

A Listen, point, and say. CD2 34

1	2	3	4	5
 1:00	 1:15	 1:30	 1:45	 2:00
one o'clock	one fifteen	one thirty	one forty-five	two o'clock

38

B Listen and find. CD2 35

C Listen and say. Then practice. CD2 36

It's | one o'clock.
    | one fifteen.

It's = It is

1.

2. 1:15

3.

4. 1:45

5. 2:00

D Listen, ask, and answer. Then practice. CD2 37

What time is it? | It's one o'clock.
               | It's one fifteen

1.

2.

3.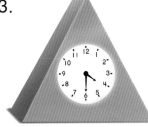

4. 4:45

5. 3:00

6. 10:30

E Look at B. Point, ask, and answer.

What time is it?

It's eleven o'clock.

What time is it now?

Lesson 2 Meals

A Listen, point, and say. CD2 38 •))

1	2	3	4
breakfast	lunch	snack	dinner

39

B Listen, ask, and answer. Then practice. CD2 39 •))

When do you eat breakfast? | I / We eat breakfast at seven o'clock.

a snack

C Listen, ask, and answer. Then practice.

| When does | he
she | eat breakfast? | He
She | eats breakfast at seven o'clock. |

1. 7:00
2. 12:30
3. 4:15
4. 7:45
5. 7:00
6. 12:45
7. 4:30
8. 6:15

D Sing.

When Do You Eat Breakfast?

When do you eat breakfast?

   I eat breakfast at 7:15.

   I like eggs and juice.

When do you eat lunch?

   I eat lunch at 1:00.

   I like soup and salad.

When do you eat dinner?

   I eat dinner at 6:45.

   French fries and spaghetti!

40

E What about you and your partner? Ask and answer.

When do you eat lunch?

I eat lunch at one o'clock.

When do you eat breakfast?

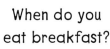

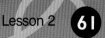

A Talk about the pictures. Then listen and read.

Time for Bed

B Listen and number. CD2 43·))

C Sing. CD2 44·))

What Time Is It?

Wake up!
   What time is it?
It's time for school.
Wake up!
It's seven thirty.
It's time for school.

Good night.
   What time is it?
It's time for bed.
Good night.
It's nine fifteen.
It's time for bed.

41

D Listen and say. Then act. CD2 45·))

What time is it?

It's eight o'clock.
It's time for bed.

It's time for a snack!

bed

2
dinner

3
school

Health

A Listen, point, and say. CD2 46

wake up

go to school

come home

go to bed

42

B Listen, ask, and answer. Then practice. CD2 47

When does | he
she | wake up?

He
She | wakes up at seven o'clock in the morning.

wake → wakes
go → goes
come → comes

in the morning

in the afternoon

in the evening

at night

7:00

8:15

6:00

8:45

C Listen, point, and say. CD2 48

eat	→ eats
play	→ plays
do	→ does
watch	→ watches

Start

9:45
go to bed

8:00
do homework

7:15
eat dinner

6:30
watch TV

5:45
play the guitar

5:00
come home

3:45
play soccer

3:15
eat a snack

12:30
eat lunch

8:15
go to school

7:30
eat breakfast

7:00
wake up

night   morning
evening   afternoon

D Look at C. Play the game.

I do homework in the afternoon. What about you?

When does he wake up?

He wakes up at seven o'clock in the morning.

E What about you? Ask and answer.

When do you come home?

I come home at three thirty in the afternoon.

8 My Week

A Listen, point, and say. CD2 49

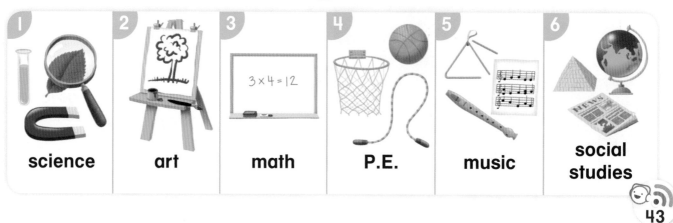

1	2	3	4	5	6
science	art	math	P.E.	music	social studies

43

B Listen and find. CD2 50

66 Unit 8

C Listen and say. Then practice. 🔊 CD2 51

His
Her | favorite subject is science.

1.
2.
3.
4.
5.
6.

D Listen, ask, and answer. Then practice. 🔊 CD2 52

What's | his / her | favorite subject?   It's science.

What's = What is
It's = It is

E Look at B. Point, ask, and answer.

What's her favorite subject?

It's math.

My favorite subject is art.

Lesson 1   **67**

A **Listen, point, and say.** CD2 53

| karate class | dance class | swimming class | English class |

Hi!

How are you?

44

B **Listen and say. Then practice.** CD2 54

Danny **goes to** karate **class on** Mondays.

1.

Monday
Danny

2.

Tuesday
Julie

3.

Wednesday
Mike

4.

Thursday
Jay

What are you wearing?

5.

Friday
Emma

6.

Saturday
Carla

C Listen, ask, and answer. Then practice. CD2 55

When does | he / she | go to karate class?

He / She | goes to karate class on Tuesdays.

	Monday	Tuesday	Wednesday	Thursday	Friday	Saturday
		① karate class		**②** swimming class	**③** dance class	
	④ karate class		**⑤** English class			**⑥** swimming class

D Sing. CD2 56

Karate Class

Sunday, Monday, Tuesday, Wednesday,
Thursday, Friday, Saturday

He goes to karate class on Mondays.

He goes to swimming class on Tuesdays.

She goes to dance class on Wednesdays.

She goes to English class on Thursdays.

45

E What about you? Tell your partner.

I go to dance class on Saturdays.

When do you go to English class?

A **Talk about the pictures. Then listen and read.** CD2 57

A Friend

Listen and number. CD2 58

C **Sing.** CD2 59

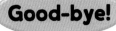
Good-bye!

What time is it?
   It's time to go.
What time is it?
   It's time to go.
Bye, bye, bye, bye.
See you. Good-bye.

46

D **Listen and say. Then act.** CD2 60

Good-bye!

Good-bye!

Good-bye!

2
See you!

3
Bye!

Do you speak English?

Lesson 3 **71**

Lesson 4 **Countries**

Social Studies

A **Listen, point, and say.** CD2 61

1	2	3	4
Brazil	**Canada**	**Egypt**	**South Korea**

47

B **Listen, ask, and answer. Then practice.** CD2 62

Where's	he she	from?	He's She's	from Brazil.

Where's = Where is
He's = He is
She's = She is

C Listen and number. CD2 63

Friend	Name	Country	Favorite subject	Class	Day
☐	Ali	Egypt	science	English	Wednesdays
☐	Becky	Canada	P.E.	karate	Tuesdays
☐	Hee-Young	South Korea	art	dance	Thursdays
☐	Bruno	Brazil	math	swimming	Mondays

D Look at C. Tell your partner. Take turns.

This is Ali. He's from Egypt. His favorite subject is science.
He goes to English class on Wednesdays.

Where are you from?

E What about you? Tell the class.

My name is [ ].

I'm from [ ].

My favorite subject is [ ].

I go to [ ] class

on [ ].

Review 4

Award

A I can say these words.

1.
2.
3.
4.
5.
6.

7. 3 × 4 = 12
8.
9.
10.
11.
12.

B I can talk about these topics.

1.
the time

2.
meals

3.
daily routine

4.
subjects

5.
classes

5.
countries

C I can talk with you.

1.

What time is it?

2.
Bye!

Phonics

A Listen, point, and say. CD2 64

rain **ai/ay** play

beach **ea/y** candy

cry **y/ie** pie

glue **ue/ui** juice

48

B Look at A. Point and read with your partner.

C Listen and read. CD2 65

1.

He can play at the beach.

2.

The glue is in the rain.

3.

She likes pie and candy.

Syllabus

Welcome

The Days of the Week: Sunday, Monday, Tuesday, Wednesday, Thursday, Friday, Saturday

What day is it today? It's Sunday.

Classroom Verbs: read, write, spell, come to the board, open your book, close your book

Unit 1 How We Feel

Lesson 1	Lesson 2	Lesson 3	Lesson 4 Science
Feelings: happy, sad, hot, cold, hungry, thirsty	**Feelings:** sick, tired, bored, excited	**Story: Are You OK?**	**The Senses:** see, hear, smell, taste, touch
I'm happy. I'm not sad. Are you happy? Yes, I am./No, I'm not.	He's/She's sick. Is he/she sick? Yes, he/she is. No, he/she isn't.	**Conversation:** Ouch! What's wrong? My leg hurts.	What can he/she see? He/She can see a bird.
		Be kind.	

Unit 2 In Town

Lesson 1	Lesson 2	Lesson 3	Lesson 4 Social Studies
Jobs: doctor, nurse, teacher, student, pilot, cook	**Jobs:** police officer, firefighter, bus driver, soccer player	**Story: Oh, Danny**	**Places:** hospital, school, home, restaurant
He's/She's a doctor. He/She isn't a nurse. Is he/she a doctor? Yes, he/she is. No, he/she isn't.	They're police officers. They aren't firefighters. Are they police officers? Yes, they are. No, they aren't.	**Conversation:** Excuse me. May I borrow your phone? Sure. Here you are. Thanks.	Where's the doctor? He's/She's at the hospital.
		Be careful.	

Review 1 Units 1 and 2   **Phonics** Bonus   cave, cub, girl, game, jam, jug, hippo, hose, king, kitten, six, box

Unit 3 Things to Eat

Lesson 1	Lesson 2	Lesson 3	Lesson 4 Science
Food: soup, salad, spaghetti, french fries, steak, eggs	**Fruit:** apple, banana, orange, peach	**Story: Yes, Please**	**Dairy Products:** milk, yogurt, cheese, butter
What do you want? I want soup. I don't want soup. What does he/she want? He/She wants soup. He/She doesn't want soup.	I have/don't have apples. He/She has apples. He/She doesn't have apples. Do you have apples? Yes, I do./No, I don't. Does he/she have apples? Yes, he/she does. No, he/she doesn't.	**Conversation:** Do you want an apple? Yes, please. No, thank you.	Do you like milk? Yes, I do. No, I don't.
		Be polite.	

Unit 4 Things to Wear

Lesson 1	Lesson 2	Lesson 3	Lesson 4 Social Studies
Clothes: shirt, dress, skirt, pants, socks, shoes	**Clothes:** cap, T-shirt, shorts, sneakers	**Story: Where's Mom?**	**Clothes:** hat, coat, sweater, boots
What's he/she wearing? He's/She's wearing a white shirt and gray pants.	What are you wearing? I'm wearing a red cap and green shorts./We're wearing red caps and green shorts.	**Conversation:** What's your phone number? It's 555-0182.	Is he/she wearing a hat? Yes, he/she is. No, he/she isn't.
		Be safe.	

Review 2 Units 3 and 4   **Phonics** Bonus   black, blob, clock, clam, flag, fly, brush, bread, crib, crayon, frog, friend

Unit 5 Things to Do

Lesson 1	Lesson 2	Lesson 3	Lesson 4
Actions: read, write, draw, talk, sing, dance What are you doing? What's he/she doing? I'm/He's/She's reading. I'm not writing. He/She isn't writing.	**Actions:** eat, drink, sleep, play What are you/they doing? We're/They're eating. We/They aren't drinking.	**Story: Let's Play!** **Conversation:** Let's play! Good idea! Be nice.	**Activities:** play the guitar, listen to music, watch TV, do homework Is he/she playing the guitar? Yes, he/she is. No, he/she isn't. Are they playing the guitar? Yes, they are./No, they aren't.

Unit 6 Home

Lesson 1	Lesson 2	Lesson 3	Lesson 4
Things at Home: bed, bookshelf, table, sofa, clock, computer There's a bed next to the bookshelf. Is there a bed next to the bookshelf? Yes, there is./No, there isn't.	**Rooms:** bedroom, bathroom, living room, kitchen There's one bed in the bedroom. There are two beds in the bedroom. Are there two beds in the bedroom? Yes, there are./No, there aren't.	**Story: Surprise!** **Conversation:** The living room's messy! Let's clean up. OK. Be helpful.	**Numbers:** 0–100 How many pencils are there? There are 24 pencils.

Review 3 Units 5 and 6   **Phonics** sheep, shell, chair, chin, three, think, whale, wheel, phone, photo

Unit 7 My Day

Lesson 1	Lesson 2	Lesson 3	Lesson 4
Time: one o'clock, one fifteen, one thirty, one forty-five, two o'clock What time is it? It's one o'clock. It's one fifteen.	**Meals:** breakfast, lunch, snack, dinner When do you eat breakfast? I/We eat breakfast at seven o'clock. When does he/she eat breakfast? He/She eats breakfast at seven o'clock.	**Story: Time for Bed** **Conversation:** What time is it? It's eight o'clock. It's time for bed. Be healthy.	**Daily Routine:** wake up, go to school, come home, go to bed When does he/she wake up? He/She wakes up at seven o'clock in the morning.

Unit 8 My Week

Lesson 1	Lesson 2	Lesson 3	Lesson 4
Subjects: science, art, math, P.E., music, social studies His/Her favorite subject is science. What's his/her favorite favorite subject? It's science.	**Classes:** karate class, dance class, swimming class, English class Danny goes to karate class on Mondays. When does he/she go to karate class? He/She goes to karate class on Tuesdays.	**Story: A Friend** **Conversation:** Good-bye! See you! Bye! Be friendly.	**Countries:** Brazil, Canada, Egypt, South Korea Where's he/she from? He's/She's from Brazil.

Review 4 Units 7 and 8   **Phonics** rain, play, beach, candy, cry, pie, glue, juice

Word List

A

a. 2
about 7
actions 40
activities 46
afternoon 64
am 5
an 25
and 2
apple 24
apples 24
are 3
aren't 14
art 66
at 16

B

ball 10
banana 24
bananas 24
bathroom 50
be 8
beach 75
bed 48
bedroom 50
beds 50
behind 49
bike 2
bird 10
black 33
blob 39
blue 33
board 3
book 3
books 52
bookshelf 48
bookshelves 50
boots 36
bored 6
borrow 16
box 21
Brazil 72
bread 11
breakfast 60
brother 2
brothers 2
brush 39
bus 11
bus driver 14
bus drivers 14
butter 28
bye 70

C

can 2
Canada 72
candy 75
can't 34
cap 32
caps 32
car 10
careful 16
cave 21
chair 57
chairs 50
cheese 28
chin 57
clam 39
classes 68
classroom 53
clean 52
clock 39
clocks 50
close your book 3
clothes 30
coat 36
cold 4
come home 64
come to the board 3

comes 64
comes home 64
computer 48
cook 12
countries 72
country 73
crayon 39
crib 39
cry 75
cub 21

D

dad 62
daily routine 64
dairy products 28
dance 40
dance class 68
dancing 41
Danny 2
day 3
dinner 60
do 23
doctor 12
does 23
doesn't 23
dog 2
do homework 46
doing 41
doing homework 46
doll 10
don't 2
draw 40
drawing 41
dress 30
drink 42
drinking 42

E

eat 42
eating 42
eat dinner 65
eats 61
eggs 22
Egypt 72
eight 2
eighteen 54
eighty 54
eleven 54
Emma 2
English 70
English class 68
evening 64
excited 6
excuse 16

F

fast 2
father 13
favorite 67
feelings 4
fifteen 54
fifty 54
find 34
finger 9
fingers 53
firefighter 14
firefighters 14
five 54
flag 39
flower 10
fly 39
food 22
for 62
forty 54
four 54
fourteen 54
french fries 22
Friday 3
friend 31
friendly 70

frog 39
from 72
fruit 24
furniture 56

G

game 21
girl 21
glue 75
go 8
goes 64
goes to bed 64
goes to school 64
goes to work 65
good 44
good-bye 70
go to bed 64
go to school 64
go to work 64
gray 31
green 2

H

hand 9
hands 53
happy 4
has 24
hat 36
have 2
he 7
head 33
hear 10
hello 70
helpful 52
her 34
here 16
he's 6
hi 44
hippo 21
his 67
home 18
homework 46
hose 21
hospital 18
hot 4
how 54
hungry 4
hurts 8

I

I 2
ice cream 10
idea 44
I'm 2
in 3
in front of 49
is 2
isn't 7
it 3
it's 2

J

jam 21
job 70
jobs 12
jug 21
juice 10
Julie 2

K

karate class 68
kind 8
king 21
kitchen 50
kite 10
kitten 21
kittens 21
know 52

L

leg 8
let's 44
like 2
likes 39
listening to music . . . 46
listen to music 46
living room 50
look 16
lunch 60

M

many 54
marker 17
math 66
may 16
me 16
meals 60
meet 70
messy 52
Mike 2
milk 28
Mom 16
Monday 3
morning 64
mother 34
music 66
my 2

N

name 2
new 44
next to 49
nice 44
night 62
nine 2
nineteen 54
ninety 54
no 5
not 5
now 43
number 34
numbers 54
nurse 12

O

oh 8
OK 8
on 21
one 50
one fifteen 58
one forty-five 58
one hundred 54
one o'clock 58
one thirty 58
oops 9
open your book 3
orange [fruit] 24
orange [color] 33
oranges 24
ouch 8

P

pants 30
peach 24
peaches 24
P.E. 66
pen 11
pencil case 55
pencils 54
phone 16
photo 57
pie 75
pilot 12
pink 34
pizza 2
places 18
play 2
playing 42
playing the guitar 46

play the guitar 46
please 17
police officer 14
police officers 14
polite 26

R

rain 75
read 3
reading 41
ready 8
red 33
restaurant 18
room 51
rooms 50

S

sad 4
safe 29
salad 22
Saturday 3
school 18
science 66
see 10
senses 10
set 8
seven 3
seven o'clock 60
seventeen 54
seventy 54
she 7
sheep 57
shell 57
she's 6
shirt 30
shoes 30
shorts 32
sick 6
sing 40
singing 41
sister 2
six 21
sixteen 54
sixty 5
skirt . . . .
sleep . . . .
sleeping . . . .
smell . . . .
snack 60
sneakers 32
so 8
soccer 2
soccer player 14
soccer players 14
social studies 66
sock 52
socks 30
sofa 48
sofas 50
sorry 16
soup 22
South Korea 72
spaghetti 22
speak 70
spell 3
steak 22
story 8
student 12
subject 67
subjects 66
Sunday 3
sure 16
surprise 52
sweater 36
swimming class 68

T

table 48
tables 50
talk 40

talking 41
taste 10
teacher 12
ten 54
thanks 8
thank you 16
the 3
there 3
there's 49
the time 74
they 14
they're 14
things at home 48
think 8
thirsty 4
thirteen 54
thirty 54
this 2
three 54
Thursday 3
time 58
tired 6
to 3
today 3
too 44
touch 10
trees 16
T-shirt 32
T-shirts 32
Tuesday 3
twelve 54
twenty 54
twenty-five 54
two 2
two o'clock 58

U

under 52
up 52

W

wake 64
wakes 64
wakes up 64
wake up 64
want 23
wants 23
watching TV 46
watch TV 46
we 32
wearing 31
Wednesday 3
week 3
we're 32
whale 57
what 3
what's 8
wheel 57
when 60
where 18
where's 18
white 31
whoa 16
winning 44
wow 52
write 3
writing 41
wrong 8

Y

yellow 31
yes 5
yogurt 28
you 5
your 3
you're 17

Z

zero 54